The Lost Candy Bar

"*The Lost Candy Bar appeals to kids of all ages. It is a family story with the excitement of surviving a fishing trip, but losing the treat of the day. Steve Kihm relates to the kids. I highly recommend his book.*"

Jackie Meyer, Elementary School Library Media Specialist

"*Steve visited our school on Read Across America Day, and shared his story. It's a wonderful book for both children and adults. I also feel that it's a great read for older students who are struggling readers because the layout of the book is not like that of a conventional chapter book.*"

Stephanie Seffrood, Elementary School Reading Specialist

"*The Lost Candy Bar is a refreshing story for all children to enjoy. The humor and real life experience makes this book a fun read in the classroom. Reading The Lost Candy Bar is a must for elementary classrooms.*"

Michele Bemke, Elementary School Teacher

"*If you have a youngster between the ages of 6-9 and finding a book he will read has become a difficult chore, you may have just found a solution to your problem if you pick up a copy of The Lost Candy Bar.*"

★★★★★ **Reader Views**

"*This very funny and charmingly written little story from the author's own childhood will be especially entertaining for young readers ages 6 to 9, particularly any young boys who don't particularly care to read books for pleasure!*"

★★★★★ **Midwest Book Review**

Illustrated by tom lowes

Steve Kihm

Published by

Steve Kihm

www.thelostcandybar.com

Printed in the United States by

Kramer Printing

Westport, WI

ISBN: 1-59598-013-X

LCCN: 2004112506

Quantity discounts available.

Third printing, 2006.

DEDICATION

To my all-time
favorite
snack…

HERSHEY'S

Chocolate Bar

ACKNOWLEDGMENTS

My appreciation goes to
Kira Henschel and Robin Willard
for helping me to produce this wonderful book.

I also appreciate the efforts of Tom Lowes, whose
artwork alone justifies the price of the book.

Janet Pulvermacher's creativity
in laying out the book is awe inspiring.

I am grateful to Kristin Jackson for arranging
substantially more book publicity than I ever
imagined was possible, and to
Teri Gehin for her innovative graphic design efforts.

Thanks also to Patricia King for her
insightful legal advice.

Special thanks to all the people
who encouraged and supported me
in this endeavor.

Finally, thanks again to my mom,
who made me go fishing.

THE LOST CANDY BAR

When I was nine years old, I was sitting at home one summer day and the phone rang. My mom answered.

"Hello," she said. Then she said, "Just a minute. I'll get him."

I wondered just who
she was going to get.

it soon became clear that it was me.

"Your grandpa wants to know
if you want to go fishing with him,"
said my mom.

Grandpa… was my dad's dad.
I was kind of afraid of my grandpa

because...

he was real loud and rough.

I was a

very quiet little boy

who **never** did anything wrong…

okay...

so I **maybe**

did a **few** things wrong,

but,...

they weren't really my fault!

I really didn't want to go fishing,

but,...

I could see that my mom

wanted me to go.

"Talk to Grandpa Leo," said my mom.

"Hello,"

I said softly.

"Steve, this is Grandpa…you want to go fishing with me today?" he asked.

"I don't know if I can. Let me ask my mom," I said.

Now everybody knows when kids

say,...

"I don't know, let me ask my mom,"

they **really** mean

"I don't want to go"

because,...

if they **really** wanted

to go they would just say

yes!

and skip the mom part.

I wanted my mom

to say no…

because...

I was

afraid

to go out in the boat

with Grandpa by myself.

As it would turn out,

I was correct to be a little scared.

My mom said, "You go fishing with your grandpa. **It will be good for you.**"

Everybody

also knows

when your mom says…

"**it will be good for you,**"

you know it's probably

not,…

going to be much

fun!

So I said in my soft little
nine-year-old voice,
"I guess I can go."

"Good," said my grandpa.
"Have your dad bring you over
and we'll go out on the boat."

That...

wasn't what I wanted to hear.

You see...

Grandpa Leo was

kind of wild sometimes

and...

I was **afraid**

he might

crash his boat into

somebody or something.

I wished we could just fish off the shore.

But no,...

we were going out

on the mighty Mississippi River.

The Mississippi is a very large river,
one of the biggest in the world.
It flows from Minnesota all the way to
the Gulf of Mexico.

I always thought that if I fell in the
river I would end up in
New Orleans, or at least St. Louis.

In some places the river is very deep.

It was kind of a scary place for me to be, even when I was with my dad—he was only half as wild as my grandpa.

The water is dark brown with little green things floating in it.

I was

not,...

happy about this fishing trip!

But,...

all that changed when my mom went to the cupboard in the back closet.

Good things were kept back there.

Things my brother and

five

sisters (yes, I have five sisters)

could not take

without permission.

My mom came out of the back closet

and said, "I'll pack you a lunch.

You can have one of these."

My heart nearly stopped!

When I was little,

we didn't have a lot of money.

So treats…such as

Candy Bars

were reserved for special occasions like

when you were born or when you died.

This,...

changed everything!

I did not know that the trip would

involve me getting to eat

a whole

HERSHEY®s candy bar.

I was READY to go fishing!

My mom put a peanut butter and jelly sandwich and an orange along with the candy bar in my little metal lunch box.

She handed it to me and said, "Here you go. Have fun."

I always wondered

why,...

my mom had to order me to have fun.

Did she think I would

forget,...

to have fun if she didn't tell me?

I wasn't sure.

My dad came in from the garden.
He said, "I'm going to take you over to
Leo's." My dad always called his dad
"Leo" instead of "Dad," which was
kind of funny to me. So we drove over
to Grandpa Leo's. It was only about

two miles so it didn't take long.

I sat with my precious lunch box

on my lap and looked out the car

window as we drove.

My grandpa lived less than a block

from the river. My dad had

grown up in that house.

My dad liked to hunt and fish a lot.

He lived in the perfect place for that.

Grandpa's house, well now

that,...

was not so perfect!

It was built on top of a place
that used to be a landfill—a place
where they dumped garbage!

Over time the house started to sink into
the ground as the garbage underneath
rotted away. But one side of the
house sank more than the other,
so the house was tilted to one side.
You could actually put a ball in the
middle of the living room and it would
not stay there—it would roll to one side
of the room. We liked playing with
balls in Grandpa's house.

Grandma Emmy was always in the
house. She was also always baking.
She loved cakes and cookies.
She hated vegetables.

I always wanted to live with her because
the only things we ever ate when we
went there were
cake and cookies.

Of course to wash it all down...
we drank soda pop.
My dad pulled into the driveway and
Grandpa Leo came out to see us.
"I've got the boat down by the pier,"
said Grandpa.

My dad said, "Do you have that
new anchor system on the boat?"

"Yep," said Grandpa.

What...

new anchor system?"

I said to myself.

You see, I

knew

that any kind of

new equipment on the boat

was just one more thing

that could get us into trouble.

I didn't know what

a new anchor system was,

but...

I didn't like the sound of it.

We went down to the boat.
The new anchor system was one
that allowed my grandpa to drop and
raise the boat's anchor without
moving around in the boat.

First,...

I thought

'That's good!'

I hated it when somebody

moved around in the boat

because...

the boat

would tip from side to side.

So...

if Grandpa could drop and raise

the anchor

without leaving his seat

that...

would eliminate

the rocking problem.

But before I was able to get too calm
I heard something that I knew was
not a good sign. My dad said to
my grandpa, "Now if the anchor rope
gets stuck, don't stand up to
try to loosen it because
you'll slip and fall into the river."

Great,...

I knew what that meant—the

anchor rope

would probably get stuck...

Grandpa would stand up...

and,...

he'd fall into the river...

Then,...

I would have to

live the rest of my life…

on an island in the

middle of the Mississippi River.

I had to make a quick decision.

If,...

I really didn't want to go fishing,

I could tell my dad

and,...

he would take me home.

But,...

I knew that if I went home

then,...

my mom would put the

HERSHEY'S chocolate bar

back in the closet

and one of my sisters

would probably eventually get it.

I thought for a second and then decided
that I was going to be the one to eat
that candy bar. So when my grandpa
said, "Are you ready to go?"

I said

in my little soft voice,

"I guess so."

I was in the front of the boat and
my grandpa was in back by the motor.

I looked straight ahead
as we headed out on the river.

I looked back for a second to
see my dad. But I was too scared
to wave. We went around the
bend in the river and my dad
disappeared from view.

You might wonder

why...

I was scared.

I forgot to tell you

one tiny little detail.

I couldn't swim—at least not very well!

And we were headed
for Goose Island.

The water near there was
very deep—about 40 feet in some
places. I was too young to realize
that for a person who can't swim,
it doesn't matter if the water is

6 feet deep or 40 feet deep—if
you fall in you're going to drown.

But,...

I thought

in the 40-foot-deep part

there probably was a

monster

at the bottom

ready to eat me after I drowned!

So,...

I decided

that drowning in 6 feet

of water would be a lot better!

We got to Goose Island and Grandpa shut off the motor. He pulled the rope on the automatic anchor machine and the anchor went to the bottom of the river. The anchor was attached to the boat by the rope. Using the anchor allowed us to stay in one place on the river. If we didn't have an anchor we would have drifted with the river current.

Without the anchor we probably would have ended up in New Orleans, or at least St. Louis... no matter what happened I was sure that I would eventually end up in one of those places!

We fished for awhile but we didn't get a single bite. So Grandpa said, "Let's try another spot."

Great!

That was the last thing
I wanted to hear!

That...

meant we were
going to have to
pull up the anchor
and drive to another spot.

I was afraid that the anchor rope
would get stuck, Grandpa would
stand up to try to fix it, and
then he would fall into the water.
So as my grandpa started to pull the
anchor rope I closed my eyes and
held on to my precious lunch box.

I was going to protect my
HERSHEY'S candy bar
no matter what happened.

Well Grandpa pulled and the anchor
came up just like it was supposed to.
I opened one eye to see if Grandpa
had fallen into the water.

He hadn't!

I opened the other eye.

Hey...

we were okay.

This fishing trip was
going to be fun after all.

But I spoke too soon. Grandpa drove the boat next to a little island. He shut off the motor. Then he pulled the anchor rope to release the anchor into the river. The anchor didn't move.

Oh oh,...

So…Grandpa pulled harder.

The anchor didn't move.

This was not good!

So…Grandpa pulled even harder.

The anchor still didn't move.

I hoped that Grandpa would say,

"Well, I guess we have to go

home now since the anchor

machine is broke and

I don't want to stand up

to pull on the rope real hard

because I'll probably

fall into the water."

I figured that we had been out

long enough that I would

be able to keep

my candy bar.

Well, unfortunately,

Grandpa didn't say that.

In fact he didn't say anything.

What did Grandpa do?

You got it!

He stood up…

and pulled on the rope

real hard.

The next thing I heard was a big splash.

Without even turning to look I knew

that Grandpa had fallen into the river.

Then I heard Grandpa holler,

"Get to the shore!"

I jumped from the boat into the

water next to the little island.

We were close enough that

I could dog paddle safely to the land.

I got out of the water and
realized that I had made a
huge mistake.

I had left my lunch box
with my HERSHEY'S candy bar on the
boat when I jumped out.

"Oh no,...
My candy bar!"
I said to myself.

I thought for a second, then determined
that my candy bar would be fine since it
was still in the boat. I quickly realized,
however, that we had a bigger problem.

When Grandpa, who was still in the water, had fallen out of the boat into the river, he actually had pulled the back end of the boat under the water with him.

The boat was sinking.

I stood on the shore and watched the boat, along with my lunch box, sink slowly into the Mississippi River.

Grandpa, who could swim (sort of), worked his way to the shore.

There we were

in the middle of

nowhere...

with a boat underwater.

My lunch box was

now underwater too.

Grandpa and I were

both dripping wet.

I thought for a moment and decided that

everything...

was my mom's fault

all because...

she made me

go on the fishing trip.

Grandpa realized that we
had a much larger problem.
"How the heck are we going
to get back to the city?"
he wondered out loud as
he stood there in his
soggy clothes.

But before I even had time to
get scared a big fishing boat
appeared out of nowhere.

My grandpa flagged the driver down.
He was a commercial fisherman—a
person who catches fish and sells
them for money. He picked us up and
took us back to the city. He was nice.

My grandpa changed his clothes and
drove me—still in my wet clothes,
back home.

My mom saw me walking up the
driveway and came running out and
said, "What happened to you?"

I was still mad at her for making me
go fishing with Grandpa
so I didn't say anything.

My grandpa explained what happened.
My mom told my grandpa that
everything was okay because
both of us were safe.

Now...

I don't know where moms

get these crazy ideas,

but...

everything was

not okay.

My precious HERSHEY'S candy bar

was sitting at the bottom

of the Mississippi River!

How,...

could that be ok?

I thought the fish

would probably eat it

if,...

they could figure out how

to open my lunch box.

It was clear that I would

never,...

see my candy bar again.

Or would I?

The next morning my dad woke me up. "Get up" he said. "You, me, Uncle Norm, and Grandpa are going to get the boat."

So I got dressed and off we went in my dad's boat right back to the place that I was so glad to get away from the day before. But this was safer. We were going in the big boat and my dad and my uncle were along.

That way...

if my grandpa fell in again,

they...

could deal with him.

It was really cool the way they rescued the boat. The boat was only partially submerged. They tied a rope on it and pulled it out of the water with the big boat. We went real fast and the water in my grandpa's boat was sucked out of holes in the back of his boat.

In a matter of just a few minutes Grandpa's boat was floating on the surface again, good as ncw.

Well, almost.

What none of us had realized up until that point was that when the boat went under the water, it had rolled on its side.

42

Everything in the boat (fishing poles, oars, and most importantly, my lunch box) was still underwater.

My lunchbox was gone.

So was my candy bar!

At least I thought it was.
My dad always had the best ideas.
Without saying much, my uncle and my dad got out fishing poles.

"Are you going fishing now?"
I asked.

"I guess we are," said my dad, "but we're not going after fish." Then I looked at the hooks on the fishing poles. They were **huge** hooks. There was no bait on the hook. My dad threw his fishing line into the water.

The hook went down...
My dad reeled the line in.

I couldn't believe it!

My dad had hooked one of Grandpa's fishing poles that was lying on the bottom of the river. He put it in the boat. My uncle then threw his fishing line in the water. He pulled up my grandpa's seat cushion off the bottom of the river.

Now,...

you have to realize that
they were pulling these things
off the bottom of the river
that was 40 feet down.

They couldn't see

anything!

They just tossed their lines in
and pulled.

Up came most of the stuff we had in
Grandpa's boat the day before.

As I was watching with
amazement my heart jumped.
My uncle had hooked
my lunch box
by its handle and was
pulling it toward the boat!

"My candy bar!"

I yelled.

"What are you yelling about?"
my dad asked.

"There's a HERSHEY®S candy bar
in my lunch box," I explained.

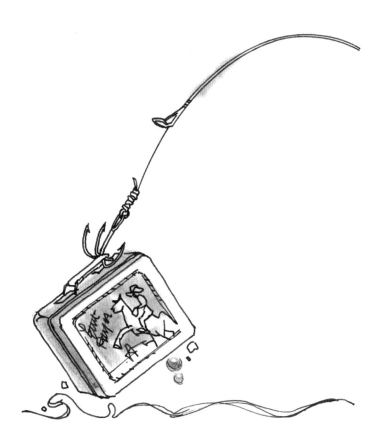

My dad and my uncle laughed.
My uncle said, "Well that candy bar
was sitting at the bottom of the
river all night long.
There won't be much left of it."

I wanted to see for myself.
So as the lunch box was put into
the boat I opened it up.

Well, one thing was clear—a peanut
butter and jelly sandwich wrapped in
cellophane doesn't look at all like a
peanut butter and jelly sandwich
after spending a night on the
bottom of the river.

My orange didn't fare much better.

It was shriveled and had a funny color.

But,...

my candy bar

looked perfectly preserved!

It was even still in its wrapper!

I was glad that the

fish hadn't gotten it.

I opened the wrapper expecting to see
my rich milk chocolate HERSHEY'S
candy bar just waiting to be eaten.

I was shocked!

Just when I thought I was going
to get to eat my long-lost
HERSHEY®S candy bar, I couldn't.

The river had teased me.

It gave me back
my candy bar, but it
took the chocolate out of it.

I was sad.

Then I had a brilliant idea.

Maybe...

the river just took

the **color** out of the candy bar.

Maybe...

it still

tasted

like a HERSHEY'S candy bar.

It was worth a try.

So...

when

no one was looking

I took a bite of that

funny looking white candy bar.

It was the

best...

tasting candy bar

I ever had!

I took another bite.

It was so good.

I ate the whole

white candy bar…

the one that had been

at the bottom of the river all night.

Life...
was good!

I was

so glad,...

that my mom

had made me

go fishing!